Petals in the Breeze

Zia Marshall

BookLeaf Publishing

India | USA | UK

Petals in the Breeze © 2024 Zia Marshall

All rights reserved.

No part of this publication may be reproduced, stored in a retrieval system, or transmitted, in any form or by any means, electronic, mechanical, photocopying, recording or otherwise, without the prior written permission of the presenters.

Zia Marshall asserts the moral right to be identified as the author of this work.

Presentation by *BookLeaf Publishing*

Web: www.bookleafpub.com

E-mail: info@bookleafpub.com

ISBN: 9789360944292

First edition 2024

*I dedicate these verses to the rustling leaves
and dancing petals, to the earth and the sky —
for they provided the canvas upon which these
verses could be painted.*

ACKNOWLEDGEMENT

To my Guru, my beacon guiding me through both stormy seas and calm waters of life.

To my family, your love has been my eternal anchor in everything I undertake.

To my son, for your endless patience and this beautiful book cover.

To my daughter, for lending your artistic eye to the illustrations and layout.

To my friends, who have been there for me through days of both sunshine and storm clouds, thank you.

To the Himalayan Writing Retreat and the vibrant bunch of writers and poets from the First Draft Club, Verse Voyages and Ink and Quill Collective, a big thank you for information, inspiration and community.

To my readers, whose hearts and minds I hope to touch with these words, thank you for embarking on this journey with me. May these verses resonate with you, inspire you, and remind you of the beauty and wonder that surrounds us each and every day.

PREFACE

With each turn of the page, I invite you to slow down, breathe deeply, and savor the beauty of the world around you. I hope these verses offer comfort and inspiration as you navigate the complexities of life, reminding you that even in the darkest of times, there is always light waiting in the gentle flutter of the petals in the breeze.

TABLE OF CONTENTS

A Rainbow of Emotions

The Welcome Visitor

I was drinking tea the other
morning; watching sunbeams
slant through the leaves.

She came in silently, uninvited,
unnoticed and slid her arms
around me in a delicious hug.

Her name was Joy.

I hope she stays with me for a while.

My Memory Drawer

I placed my memories in a little drawer
and threw in keepsakes for good measure.
Photos with curled edges, scrawled lines on
paper,
pressed flowers in books — life's little treasures.
Future keepsakes for she who lights my life with
laughter.

Many, many moons later…

On a rainy Sunday afternoon,
picture her browsing through our treasures,
a whimsical smile lighting up her dear face,
a gurgling face beaming up at her dreamy gaze.

And I am holding these two together
creating another memory for another future.

I Wish I Could…

I wish I could
sprinkle fairy dust on all my stories
so they could be handed down through
the dusty passages of time. And many in the
years to come would smile over them.

I wish I could
capture laughter in little bottles and
hand them to strangers with careworn faces.

I wish I could
hold all my smiles in cupped hands
and sprinkle them over crying babies.

I wish I could
bind all my lessons in a book. Lessons
I learned from life's hard experiences
and hand them out to friends and strangers alike.

I wish I could
wrap wreaths of mirth around my mistakes
so others would not bow their heads in shame
but laugh at their foibles instead.

I wish I could…

I wish I could….

On Joy!

There is so much joy in nature!

The leaves dance with mirth.

The river bubbles joyfully
in its journey to the sea.

And in the lake,
there are swans
gliding peacefully,
almost reverentially.

I wish I could capture
a handful of joy from nature
and hold it forever in my soul.

On Hope!

Hope quivers across the world.

The trees shorn of leaves in winter
quiver with hope for spring
when they will be dressed
in their leafy green once more.

Hope smiles in the stormy skies
waiting for the clouds to part.

Hope lies in the broken heart
healing from embers of pain.

And hope is the soldier
limping home to his young wife.

Yes! The rainbow of hope spans the world.

Wind-swept Emotions

Your feelings, your emotions;
you were never meant to
hold on to them. Don't

imprison them in the fortress
of your terrors. Just like trees
welcome the wind rustling

through their leaves
and then let it go,
welcome your feelings,

allow them to pass through you
and let them go. And then tell
me how much lighter you feel!

Sunshine Souls

8

There are some souls who carry dark energy dragging it behind them like a shadow. And some souls dance on sunbeams and carry rainbow energy filling you with warmth.

The best kind of people are like sunshine – warm and fuzzy with beautiful smiles. They are always with you through all the highs and lows of life. And they have the remarkable gift of hearing you even when you don't have the words to express your grief.

Stay with those souls!

Summer Child

Swinging in the summer breeze!
Squealing with laughter, 'higher,' you plead!
Butterflies dance within you gloriously.
You glance at the distant ground giddily.

Perched at the greatest height exuberantly.
You peek at the hand that rocks you, trustingly.
Acres ahead as far as the eye can see.
Waiting for you lies your kingdom of aqua seas.

You fling out your arms joyously;
embracing the world confidently.
Wearing your Innocence like a wondrous creed.
Deceit, Deception, you are yet to learn of these!

Holding On to Transitions

And I wish to clasp close to me,
all things even as they go
through such transitions.

The rising ball of flame in morning skies;
the mysterious hush of the night;
the deep voice of thunder;
the ethereal rainbow in the waterfall;
sunflowers lilting toward the sun;
the calf that lays its head on my arm.

And the words that pass through my mind
as I try to pin them down on paper.

Night Walker

There is something mystical
about night walks. A hush
descends on the world;
birds settle into their nests.

A sudden chorus of crickets
breaks the spell of stillness.
The trees whisper their secrets
to you and as you walk, fireflies

dance ahead lighting your path.
And the moon bathes you
in its mellow healing light.
You can't see much except for

the shadows cast by trees. But your senses
come alive to the world around you.
The sweet fragrance of the Queen of the Night
wafts through the air. You are intensely

aware of the rustling palm leaves and
the sound of the sea as it
breaks against the shore. Night walks
are wonderfully soothing for the soul.

Bed Companions

Each night, when I tumble
into bed, I choose a companion
from those who people my day.

Tonight, I chose Anxiety,
or dare I say,
Anxiety chose me?

She slid into bed beside me,
resting her dark head
on my soft pillow,

slithering into my dreams
with her dismal drama webs.
I watch helplessly…

as she plants weeds in my garden
that strangle the tender buds
of Hope I have nurtured with such care.

And then, satisfied with the damage she has
wrought, I thought she would leave.

But no!

She slid into the forest
of my memories, obliterating
Laughter with gloomy clouds,

stripping foliage from trees, spinning
cobwebs over slivers of Joy; turning
my forest of memories into a nightmare.

Her companions joined her;
Worry and Doubt. And the Three
spun a spell of doom. Their incantations

rose like smoke
in the dank forest air.
I watched mesmerized

longing to leave, but
rooted to the ground
beneath my feet.

Till pink, at last, streaked the sable skies.
And Anxiety and her companions
faded into oblivion.

Today, I will choose my companions during the
day with greater care.

The Midnight Visitor

And at the cold hour of midnight,
Uncertainty visited me
on wings of doubt.

She wrapped her incertitude
around me in wreaths of mist.

I stared at the blue blinking light
by my bedside
marking the hours
as the darkness of Doubt
crawled all over my thoughts.

But when dawn stole in
almost unbidden,
it carried Hope
in the morning breeze
and banished Uncertainty
into a dark corner.

Battling Anxiety

Anxiety, a dark fog,
curls around you,
wrapping its tentacles,
choking the breath

out of you. And it
doesn't matter how much
you try to rationalize
your feelings or utter

lists of reasons why you
should stay calm.
You remain a rudderless
ship amidst a tsunami.

Life Lessons in the Blue Hills

The Orchestra

I stole a few minutes today
from the busy of the day
to escape into my cocoon of solitude.

I wanted to spend some time
savoring the sweet melody
of bird songs. I watched the robins

gathered in the meadow of wildflowers;
their voices rising in joyous symphony;
in complete accord with each other.

Accommodating…
the high notes;

the low ones;
the strains of sorrow;
some soulful;
and some raucous in their mirth.

And yet….

Despite all the disparate elements,
they still sang in complete synchronicity
with each other. Their little beaks
moved rhythmically in the cool air
as they strove so valiantly to sing on.

They were singing;
not for me;
or for you.

And what was so wonderful
was that they had no wish
to outdo one another.

They were singing
for the sheer pleasure
of being alive.

I think it is an important thing they do!

An Invitation to a Feast

I watched the pair of them
strutting in the grass near me;
their brown-speckled wings
tucked away for the moment,

as they abandoned their blue homes
and took to the green grass
in search of food. I froze
lest I startle them as they carried out

such serious work. And they marched on
through the green completely focused
on the task at hand. One wandered a little away
and came upon the bird feeder filled with grain.

I had left it out for them a few hours back.
He perched on the rim of the feeder
and raising his sharp beak in the air
called out incessantly; his chirp-chirp song

trilled through the air, speaking of discovery
and joy and food that was plentiful.
And slowly, almost magically, I watched
as his feathered friends swooped down
from their blue homes; perching on the feeder to
have their fill of the food. And then trilling their
"thank-you" to their speckled host, they departed
once more for their blue homes in the beyond.

Anonymous Shadows

When we turn the crisp black
and white pages, we read of
the shadows run amok
in the human world.

Senseless acts of violence
in an endless thread,
looping back, tearing out
the fragile heart of humanity.

And meanwhile, ominous clouds
bloated with rain race across the skies,
casting down their fury
in random symphony.

The tsunami and the fire
are immersed in their dance
of destruction; with nimble limbs
shaking the earth with ferocity.

I saw a hapless child
being swept away
by the rising river; his toys
bobbing helplessly beside him.

But when the thunder roars,
it is not for any reason; there is no history
behind its claim to violence. The rivers
don't plot to overflow; they just do.

I mean the tragic dance of nature
casts anonymous shadows on earth,
unleashing its motiveless fury
on fragile unsuspecting humanity.

But when humans cast shadows,
they are of a cold, premeditated variety
that speaks of the complete absence of love.

Oleanders

These soft, petalled beauties
enclose a world of duality.
Their delicate, blush petals
radiate beauty, delight hearts.

And in the meanwhile,
coursing through their sap
is lethal poison that can
steal lives. Often when I gaze

at the pink blooms,
I can't help but reflect
on the similar duality
hidden in some human lives.

Ruby Red, Sapphire Blue

I gaze at the roses, Ruby Red,
glistening with drops — not dew drops,
but the water I sprinkled on them
as I settled them in their new home,
the Sapphire Blue vase. I regard
my handiwork — Ruby against Sapphire;
a striking contrast in beauty!

As I lovingly stroke the soft petals,
I hear their cries of longing for
their plunging roots in moist earth;
the soft rain falling on their petals;
their home amidst the leaves;
the whisper of the wind;
the blue, cloud-filled skies.

A few days later, as the petals
slowly wither and fall away,
I wash the Sapphire vase
and tuck it away in a dark corner
of the cupboard. Now I content myself
with admiring the Ruby roses nestled
peacefully in their leafy homes.

Revelation in the Nilgiris

On a summer morning, nestled
in the lap of the blue hills,
as the cool air brushes
against my skin and my feet
dig into the dew-soaked green,
I listen to the Robin as he perches
on the branch, chirping away.

And my thoughts drift like clouds
one, two, three….

For I realize there are but three things
we need to do in this world.

To love the little hand placed
in yours trustingly;

To hold him against your heart
and love him as if your life
depended on it,
as long as he needs you;

And then to let him go….
Just let him go, let him go….

Just Me

As I walk among the trees, their tall, silver-gray
bodies give off the fragile fragrance of
eucalyptus and healing. The birds are singing a
song that is as old as the blue hills; a haunting
melody of a love, which I have discovered very
late in life.

And if I could, I would live my life all over
again; begin again. And this time,
I would focus on loving — Just Me!

The Laughing Dove

When the storm runs out of fury
and subsides into stillness,
I walk among the dripping boughs
to hear the song of the laughing dove.

I wrap my solitude around me,
a glittering jeweled cloak,
as if I were a queen. And I wait
for the song of the laughing dove.

The fears of life and death
melt into shadows of silence.
For I have known
but two things in life.

The joy coursing through my heart
when a song is born anew within me;
and the sweet song of the laughing dove!

Lessons From Little Things

In its search for food, the ant comes across a mighty log. Instead of trying to find a way over the log, the ant walks around it. The longer route is also the most effective one as it is free of hurdles. Ants know they don't always have to climb mountains to overcome hurdles. Sometimes it is simpler to find a new path.

While searching for food, ants stay together. They don't run amok in different directions. They understand strength in togetherness.

The Wise Visitor

And one day, Time visited me on wings of
precious hours. She said, "You have spent
enough hours growing up, growing wiser,
growing better. Trade in your chains of
conformity for a taste of wildness."

She commanded me to let go of it all. And when
I whispered back, I didn't know how, she said,
"Laugh often and uninhibited. Care a whit for
others' opinion and care enough about your
own. Don't be bound by schedules and routines.

Just be….
Be wild, be unruly, so that you can accept the
miracle that is life and fill your hours
with all things beautiful and meaningful."

Simplicity

You don't have to decorate the altar
with marigolds and roses;
spend hours on your knees
with folded hands.

Just hold a handful of wildflowers
and love in your heart
for the heavens above.
And a few words. They don't have

to be eloquent. A prayer isn't a race
to see who does it longest
and best. It is a doorway
into the portals of the divine.

Keep it simple!

Release

Trees shed their leaves in
September winds, reminding us
there is so much beauty in letting go of things.

To feel eternally light of all baggage;
the trauma, the grief, the whole package.

And yet the branches remain
tipped with tender shoots; offering
hope for new leaves in the coming months.

So it is with life as well. In letting go,
we make space for healing and growth.

Roots of Strength

Learning How To Be Strong

I wish someone had told me.
Explained it in detail
all the rules for being strong.

To be a rock,
immovable,
when waves crash against you.

To be a palm tree
bending impossibly in howling storm waves,
but never toppling over.

I wish I had met the rock, the tree before.
So I could have learned how to be strong.

Resilience

My heart is a weed.
My soul is a wildflower.

Both are strong enough
to combat rude hands
that tear at their roots.

And both are resilient enough
to push through
the cracks in pavements
towards the sun
even when they receive no nourishment.

Beauty in Broken Things

Trees crash during a storm
but they leave
upended roots
and seedlings for growth.

Rain-laden, gray clouds
burst forth with fury
and then form white, feathery puffs
drifting off into the azure blue.

And you! Yes, you!
You have broken
a thousand times
and yet here you stand.

Mother Nature knows
how to rise
from her brokenness each time
and so do you!

Voice of Love

Some days love was the sweet song of the lark at dawn.

Some days it was the wide arc of the eagle in the blue beyond.

And some days it was the little chip-chip of the green warble saying, "I'll try again tomorrow."

Chrysalis

We are all caterpillars!

Somewhat soft,
somewhat wrinkled,
messy, not perfect.

Digging deep within
to find the strength
to break through the chrysalis
and dance upon the beauty
of our butterfly wings!

Cloak of Survival

And she wished she knew
the rules to be strong.
But there are no rules.
She is already strong.

Even when grief meets her
in a silent sorrow storm;
and she is drowning
in an endless sea of anguish.

Her fortitude lies within her
tucked away next to her courage,
and her wherewithal.

We all wear the cloak of survival differently.
On some it is a placid lake;
on others it is a tsunami out of control.

Song of Strength

You bear the scent of wildflowers
and the depth of the sea lies in your eyes.

And there are universes
woven into your soul.

Remember this when any man
tries to make you feel small
and diminishes your worth.

Self-Compassion

Please don't give up on yourself;
on all the lost parts of yourself;
the parts of yourself you don't
like anymore.

Does the sea give up during a storm?
And the sun?
It still shows up after a thunderstorm.

What I am saying is there are parts
of you that need love more than
anything else. Give them that love.

And there are parts of you that will
shatter. Please don't abandon
those broken parts of you.

My Wild Bee Garden

I gazed at the emerald green
dotted with little white
and yellow flower heads.

"We need to get the lawn mowed," he said.
I shook my head but I couldn't quite explain;
put it in so many words, my need to protect the
wildflowers from being hacked to pieces and
swallowed up in the cruel jaws of the mower.

Didn't they look pretty
adorning the emerald green?

Didn't they offer a fine feast
for the bees to sup on?

I longed to enfold them
in my protective clasp
but they shook their little
white and yellow heads sadly.

"We are the others," they whispered, "for we
always have to make room for things of beauty."
And I decided that in my garden, they would
reign supreme in all their unruly beauty.

On Resting During Storms

The butterfly rose weightless,
its wings motionless
as it floated
in the summer breeze.

When lightning struck the sky
and a summer storm
cut through the heat haze,
the butterfly glided beneath a flower cup.

It knew it needed to rest during a storm
for it couldn't get its wings wet.
As should you rest
when storms rend through your life.

I Love Summer Showers

How they show up with
unexpected suddenness;
sweeping across the parched earth;

swooping down on wings of hope
to offer a brief moment of respite
from the fiery, orange blaze.

And when dark shadows
loom over your life, don't
allow your spirit to plummet.

Instead seek tiny slivers of happiness
that light up the dark shadows
in your life, albeit briefly.

Sometimes you have to cast
your own summer showers
over your life.

Water

It flows with velvety, silken
softness in the stream.

And yet, during a storm,
how quickly water loses its softness
transforming into strong sheets of rain.

And we, who are seventy percent water,
could do well to learn from
our cousin in nature.

How to be soft!

How to be strong!

Savoring Blooms of Life

The Business of Living

Oh! How we fuss over the business of life!

While the bird just lives.
Swooping low in search of food;
gathering twigs for its nest.

I have yet to see a bird
mull over the best place
to hunt for food.

It is drawn by instinct
and the sheer joy of being alive.
What a wonderful way to live!

Appreciation

And if someone asks me what I do for a living,
I will tell them my work is to love the world.

Here the mynah,
there the morning glory
in all its withering beauty.

The stars that sweep across sable skies
and the moon that blooms into fullness
and fades into nothingness.

It is not enough you say,
this work I do.

And yet I never tire of it.
So let it be enough!

For even if my clothes are mud-stained
and my footwear worn through,
my heart is filled with gratitude
to appreciate the pure delight of such beauty.

Arms Wide Open…

I think I was born
to love the world
and all the beauty
it contains. If my arms
were wide enough
to reach out and hold
it in my grasp, I would.

But for now, I content
myself with loving
the little things that
house this beautiful world.

The sunflower turning
its black seed-face
as it worships the sun.

I caress its soft petals
and then move on.

The little shells housing
the roar of the mighty ocean
in their delicate pink curve.

I collect them in a jar
and then move on.

I don't think I can ever tire of
loving this beautiful, beautiful world.

Tree Friends

On a sun-kissed Sunday,
I hugged a tree.

And I would like to imagine
that it shook out its green, leafy hair
and hugged me back
in a promise of togetherness.

It wasn't so long ago,
you used to find me
nestled in its leafy boughs
reading a favorite book.

It's impossible to recall
the child in me
and not wish her back.

So if you choose to look for me,
you may find me perched atop a tree
or maybe beneath it reading.

Moonless Nights

And many moonless nights
I have spent by my window
admiring the diamond palette
sweeping across the inky dark.

I like moonless nights!

It gives the stars a chance
to show off their splendor
without being overshadowed
by the creamy orb.

Oasis

Today I choose to lay to rest all the demons of
ambition that race through me amok.

And the world turns on its axis as it must. The
fish swim in the aqua blue and the birds fly in
search of food.

And I! I am taking the day off quietly without a
sound. I wish to escape into stillness even if it is
for a short while.

Sipping From the Cup of Life!

And we spend so much time
trying to figure out the purpose
of our precious lives. But really,
the goal of life is to live.

Draw back those shades,
banish darkness, let in
light and air. Play
some soft music and
dance in rhythm
to the dust motes
floating in sunlight.
Dip your feet in the river;
watch the sun sink into the horizon.

Life is meant to be savored
one precious moment at a time.

Leave the negative in a dark corner
and allow only beauty
and light to enter your life.

Hygge Moments

A flower-filled meadow during a monsoon shower; waking to birdsong and flowers gently bobbing their heads in the summer breeze; watching clouds drift lazily across the morning sky as I lie on my grassy pillow; watching the twinkling star-crusted skies at night by my candle-lit window; curling up with my dog, my book and a large mug of tea.

I live for these hygge moments that wrap me in a warm cloak of coziness and contentment.

Rivers of Loss

A Journey From Loss to Healing

I traversed the black River of Loss.

The hard pebbles
dotting the riverbed
cut into my feet
till they bled freely;
the red Ribbons of Grief
pooling into
the black Waters of Loss.

But I knew I had to wade on
in the black pool; stay afloat

in darkness. And one day,
the sun would strike its golden rays
on blue waters and I would find
healing on the other side.

Thunderstorms

I love thunderstorms!

When the skies rend the world
with ominous cries, before opening up
and pouring out their fury on us.

Thunderstorms remind me
that once in a way
it is fine to live out your fury.

Even the skies shriek during storms!

Why I Love the Ocean!

It never shuns me;
whether I run towards it
strong and whole
or broken and damaged.

Its smooth, shimmering, silken waves
wash over me
in a gentle rhythm that
soothes my soul.

Unlike people
who shun the broken,
the ocean embraces them
and makes them whole.

Battling Grief

When grief stalks you, go out into the forest
and breathe in the beauty of the world.
And when dark moments envelop you, listen to
the sweet call of the mynah at dawn, trilling
through the trees, echoing through the leaves.
See how the sparrow shelters under the cupped
hood of the morning glory during a brief
summer shower. And how the sun unfailingly
shows up when clouds run dry of moisture.

There is beauty in nature that soothes our souls.
If grief still envelops you, make her
your companion and walk with her
in the fields and show her the beauty
of the little allamanda sun cups on earth
and the hydrangea bursting forth with beauty
like a million stars in the soil.

And if grief still will not cease to be your
companion, remember, sweet one, even if your
life amounts to nothing more than the nail

that holds the fence together, you are
still useful and a vital part of the universe.

Rising From Loss

Recreate yourself
from the ashes of nothing.

Light wildfires in your soul
and watch the glowing embers
wash away your trauma.

Plant wildflowers in your heart
so that it may always find
the strength to bloom
through every storm.

Quell the seas
that reside in your body
and bid the storms be calm
so that you may drag
your tattered body and soul
back to the haven of a safe harbor.

You have to recreate yourself
and then do it over and over,
till you let go of everything
that caused you terrible harm
and a new person
is born from the wreckage.

Sun-dappled Shadows

We all have painful moments in life; moments when the sun is obscured behind a miasma of somber clouds; moments when grief sucks the smile from your face; moments when life seems like an unending rat race. And there seems to be no way out.

But you need to hang in there, my friend, for life has a way of throwing out a rope just when you reach the very edge of the precipice. And then, just like that the sun bursts open on your face and the world tilts upright on its axis and things are no longer askew.

Comfort in Little Things

And on days when my trauma overwhelms me,
I take comfort in the little things.

In the rose briar that twines and tumbles over the
walls;
in the gentle sound of rain casting freshness on
earth;
in the delight of the sparrow as it pecks at the
bread I have laid out;
in the breeze whispering through the trees lulling
me to sleep.

I remember the people who love me
unconditionally and will never leave me.

And I hold my memories close to me as I
rock the waves of trauma to the shores of peace.

Sunflowers

And I love the beauty of sunflowers.

Their black-faced, yellow-petalled wings seem
to whisper secrets of a thousand things.

Secrets they have gleaned from the sun to shun
darkness; turn always to the light.

I think I would heal if I were a sunflower or
behaved like one at least!

Wistful Musing Under the Wisteria

Amor Fati!

The stones and pebbles move
with the flow of the river
so smoothly, in a seamless motion.

It never occurs to them
to move against the flow.

While we are always struggling;
always flailing against the flow of fate.

Instead of lovingly accepting what is!

The Affliction of Thinking

I wondered if the river
would meet its mother sea.

And if the sparrows
would return to their nests
before the sun slipped
below the horizon.

And if the boats
would be safe
when storms
broke out over the sea.

And if my words
would delight and
find a place
in aching hearts.

And then I gave up wondering.
Perhaps I think too much.
Perhaps I should just carry
on with the business of living.

Note to Self: Being More Mindful

So engrossed was I with the words dancing in my mind, I have not noticed so many things of late. How the mist of the waterfall throws out little rainbows before crashing down into a pool. The sweet cooing of the koel heralding the arrival of yet another shower. The softened soil after a downpour and the sun slanting in through the windows. Cooking a favorite meal for someone I love while moving in tune to music as the spices sing under my fingers. Yes, there are things I haven't noticed for a while. Most people who live with their heads in clouds of words sometimes fail to notice these things.

Who Knows?

if the butterfly regrets its brief life span?

if the moon during its waxing and waning
doesn't long for a return to its fullness of
beauty?

if the river longs for a return to its bubbling
freedom once it has submerged in the sea?

Worthwhile questions!

And I have spent long moments pondering over
them.

As should you!

Your soul will expand with curiosity if only you
allow it.

And your life will be richer for it.

We, who are so sure in our worldly ambitions,
would do well to bow humbly before the Earth
as we soak in its haunting beauty.

Life's Dualities

It is absolutely terrifying!

How some people have
weathered storms within
and reflect the calm face
of the lake without;

while others are full
of storm and fury outside
with no scars to show for it inside.

Storms of Life

A perfect day, clear skies
till…
gray clouds roll over the heavens.

Wave after wave
of gray bilious clouds threaten
the perfect brilliance of the day.

Strong winds, gusts of it,
swoop down like a dozen black crows.

And then lightning strikes
the gray, cloud-bloated skies.

Life…
good one moment
and then torn apart the next.

My life, other lives
wrecked apart;
doomed by disaster's seal.

Now the crashing sound
has risen to a crescendo
and disaster reigns supreme
in the gray, ominous skies,
splattering the world,
covering it in wet fury.

House of Denial

I lived in the house of denial for a while. It had
thick doors that hardly let the sound out and
windows that wouldn't budge, however hard I
tried to open them. I used to work in darkness in
my little house till I finally learned to burst free
and look at the morning sun full in the face.

Cocoon of Peace

Very early in the morning, I venture out into quiet solitude. I find peace here and a warm glow of belonging in the empty spaces of wilderness or nothingness. I wish I could hold on to it, whatever it is, this nameless happiness or delicious peace that settles over me in the quiet hours. Formless yet palpable, a delicate shining thing. But I know it cannot last. For I must return to the busyness of living soon.

Soft Mornings

And on soft mornings,
when the dark of the night
slips into pale, pink-hued skies,

I hug new beginnings close to me
and let go of the heartache
that beset the dark hours.

For isn't there always something
hopeful, fresh and new
about the first light?

In the meanwhile….

The clocks are ticking wildly,
almost loudly, urging me back
into the busyness of life.

But for now, I refuse
to hear the ticking.
I want to stop here

for a while and watch
the pink rinse the sky
in a hope-filled glow.

A Tale of Three Trees

I see before me three verdant trees
growing side by side in perfect harmony.

Their leaves rustle, brushing against each other;
whispering "there's sunshine enough for all, it's
never a bother."

I cannot see their roots growing deep into Earth.
But I'm sure the roots don't complain "stay
away from my turf."

I think I am going to run out and hug these
mighty, humble trees.

Night Skies

My head is filled with
so much clamor!

Words, letters, sentences
all jostle for space
in my mind-head.

How then can I remain still
and contemplate the sheer beauty;
the vast silence of this star-studded sky?

As I gaze at the diamond palette radiating beauty
without uttering a single syllable, I long to
empty my mind of the words that relentlessly
swarm within me.

I walk to the edge of the cliff; I release all the
words from my crowded mind space. There they
go, floating down into blank nothingness.

Oh! What peace fills my soul!
What joy is this that settles over me
as I savor the blank canvas of my mind!

Does it match the silent beauty of the night sky?

And then as the first drops of rain fall over me,
the spell is broken.

I hurry back….

And in the meanwhile, the night
awakens to its own chorus. The rain
splashes into inky pools on the black fields.

The wind rustles among the ghostly
pear-shaped canopies. Clouds swallow
the stars as they race across sable skies.

Their silent, twinkling beauty
enveloped in the sudden storm fury
that shatters the stillness of the night skies.

And I, ensconced in my desk by the window,
hear the nightly symphony as words
like gifts drift across my mind once more.

And I smile wistfully as I recall
the fleeting beauty
of the pure, deep stillness

In the night skies…

In my mind…

Unrequited Love

I wonder what became of the flowers I gave you.
I had gathered them myself in armfuls. The
sweet aroma of summer rain rising from them as
they glistened with dew drops.

You accepted them with an enigmatic smile.
But after…. Did you carelessly toss them
on the ground? Or did you thrust them in water
in a forgotten, dark corner of your room?

My tears fell like rain that day. Did you
carelessly tread over my tears like you did the
flowers? I drink from the bitter cup of regret.
The flowers would have been happier bobbing
their heads in the summer rain.

And so would I have been happier
showering my love on them instead.

Yin and Yang

And if love makes me as fierce as a lion,
it also makes me as tender as a newborn lamb.

And if love blows over me like a hurricane,
it also settles in my being like the soft whisper
of the wind.

And it is these dualities in love that I both
oppose and welcome in equal measure.

Death of a Friend

I struck out one day in search
of my old childhood haunts.
I am not sure why exactly.

Perhaps I wished to capture, for a few moments,
the joy, the ecstasy of my innocence
before the years of experience stole it away.

I came upon the tree on which I had
once carved out my initials. But instead of the
shady green canopy under which I had spent

many happy hours reading, I was met with dried
leaves and withered branches. I wrapped my

arms around my old tree friend with sorrow for I
knew he didn't have long left; I ran my fingers
over the carved initials, knowing my children,
other children would never see them and come

to know the tree for who he was, a friend, a
shady companion, who offered me a glimpse of
heaven. And I grieved in silence as I held
the once sturdy, now peeling bark of his trunk.

What precisely did I grieve for?
For the tree?
Or for the children
who will, perhaps, never know
the joy of sleeping
under shady canopies?

On Happiness

Every morning, a brand new world is created as
the sun casts its orange glow on a new day and
the coals of darkness tumble into light. And as if
by magic, the black cloth of the lake turns blue
on which are strewn pink lotus flowers floating
on their green island-homes.

And if fate has decreed a portion of happiness in
your life, you will spend hours watching the soft
trails of pink in the azure blue.

But if thorns of despair fall within your lot and
you go through the plodding, dreary, endless
motions of life, perhaps — just perhaps, if you
stop for a moment, you will see the splendor of
the pond with its lavish lotus carpet like a breath
of fresh air reminding you there is so much
beauty in life.

And if you so dare, you, yes even you, can be
happy!

African Parrot

At times, my flower-filled heart
betrays me. Or perhaps,
it is not so much my heart
as my desire to fit in; to belong.

I gaze at the majestic red feathers;
its wings folded in useless inactivity
behind the iron bars.

Its sharp eyes bore into me.

Is it a plea;
or a command?
To fling open the cage;
release him from captivity!

But my courage fails me
and I walk on leaving him behind;
a showpiece for thoughtless humans.

The moment is lost forever…

I often think of him;
the scarlet-feathered beauty.
Why didn't I open the cage
and send him into his blue-green home
where he truly belonged?

Where, if I am honest,
I belong as well;
where I don't need to struggle
to fit in;
where I can just be.

A Timeless Tale

And when I am no longer here,
perhaps I will be missed
for a day,
or longer,
till grief is swallowed
in the everyday motions of life
and I slowly fade into
the dim recesses of memory.

You won't find me here
among the people
I used to call home.

I prefer to drift across the world.
I can trust it to continue

shining in all its splendor
even when I am no longer here
to record its beauty.

There lies the tree
I used to read beneath;
the flowers I had
tended with so much care.
I watch as the bees
swoop down on them for honey.

The mulberries
adorn the trees;
their red berries
festive against the green.

The crow swoops low,
flying past me.
He doesn't see me
for I am now a shadow
in this world,
but it is still so beautiful

www.ingramcontent.com/pod-product-compliance
Lightning Source LLC
LaVergne TN
LVHW011033200726
843509LV00011B/1267